A Showcase of Artwork and Writings by North Carolina's Children

Xanadu
The Imaginary Place

With a Story by **Dr. John Hope Franklin**
Edited by **Maya Ajmera and Olateju Omolodun**

Major Support for This Project Was Provided By

A. J. Fletcher Foundation, Cannon Foundation, Duke Energy Foundation, Grace Jones Richardson Trust, Z. Smith Reynolds Foundation

With Additional Support From
Duke University, Futures Fund of the Wildacres Leadership Initiative,
Kenan Ethics Program at Duke University, Mary Duke Biddle Foundation,
Moore & Van Allen, PLLC, North Carolina Public Allies, Perkins Library at Duke University,
Reichhold Chemicals, Sprint Mid-Atlantic

SHAKTI for *Children*

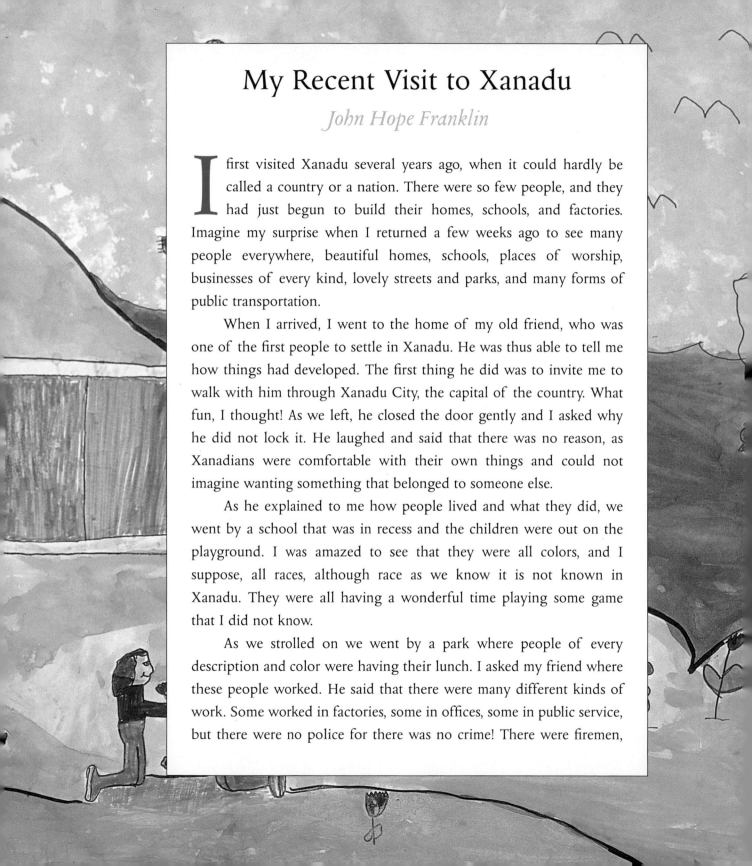

My Recent Visit to Xanadu

John Hope Franklin

I first visited Xanadu several years ago, when it could hardly be called a country or a nation. There were so few people, and they had just begun to build their homes, schools, and factories. Imagine my surprise when I returned a few weeks ago to see many people everywhere, beautiful homes, schools, places of worship, businesses of every kind, lovely streets and parks, and many forms of public transportation.

When I arrived, I went to the home of my old friend, who was one of the first people to settle in Xanadu. He was thus able to tell me how things had developed. The first thing he did was to invite me to walk with him through Xanadu City, the capital of the country. What fun, I thought! As we left, he closed the door gently and I asked why he did not lock it. He laughed and said that there was no reason, as Xanadians were comfortable with their own things and could not imagine wanting something that belonged to someone else.

As he explained to me how people lived and what they did, we went by a school that was in recess and the children were out on the playground. I was amazed to see that they were all colors, and I suppose, all races, although race as we know it is not known in Xanadu. They were all having a wonderful time playing some game that I did not know.

As we strolled on we went by a park where people of every description and color were having their lunch. I asked my friend where these people worked. He said that there were many different kinds of work. Some worked in factories, some in offices, some in public service, but there were no police for there was no crime! There were firemen,

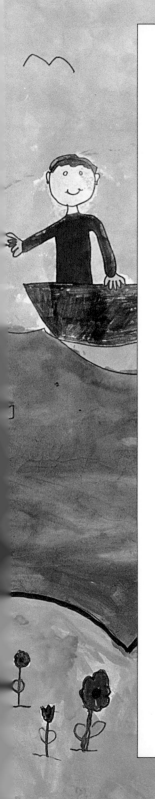

telephone repairmen, and a few automobile mechanics. Not many people had automobiles, and they did not seem to want them. Public transportation—buses and trains and airplanes—was so much better. In that way, one could travel with friends or meet people who could become friends.

It was time for us to have lunch, and my friend invited me to go with him to one of his favorite restaurants. When we arrived, I asked that we sit in a no-smoking area. That amused my friend, who informed me that there was no tobacco at all in Xanadu. It was not grown there or imported. In fact, no one smoked in Xanadu. I then told him that I was on a diet and ate no fatty foods. He said that most people in Xanadu were vegetarians, although it was possible to request meats, usually for visitors or for special occasions. We had a delicious vegetarian meal, flavored with herbs and spices from around the world. There was plenty of fruit and no artificial flavors. The meal was so satisfying.

During a pleasant afternoon in Xanadu City, we visited some workplaces, where everything was very orderly. The workers seemed so caring of each other and for their work. The workers were not exploited by their employers in any of the workplaces.

I wanted to spend more time talking and visiting the workplaces in Xanadu, but we had to rush to the airport. My friend went with me on the bus and urged me to visit Xanadu again as soon as possible. As I went through the airport, I looked for the location where security checked carry-on baggage. I asked my friend to show me to the security gate. Confused, my friend asked me why I needed a security official to check my baggage, since no weapons of any sort were allowed in Xanadu. As I boarded the plane, I assured my friend that a return visit to a place of love, justice, and tolerance would be a pleasure.

Xanadu would be like chocolate.
There is a rainbow up in the sky and
the air smells sweet like sugar.

The people in Xanadu look so pretty.
Clothes are made of gold and silver silk.
Coats are made of fake fur.

Peoples' voices would be both loud and soft.
When people sing, they clap their hands,
stomp their feet, and dance.

My favorite thing to eat in Xanadu is spaghetti.
Our family sits at the table together
and we talk about school and things that happened.
The spaghetti feels soft, fuzzy, and smooth.

Before I go to bed at night,
I brush my teeth and say my prayers.

I dream about the stars.
At night, the stars are out and it looks pretty.
The Little Dipper is beside the Mama Dipper.

——Daria Bannerman, Ebonie Boatwright, Buddy Chavis,
Andrew Daniels, Daniel Gore, Luke Huntley, Ebony Johnson,
and La'Teaya Lee, 2nd to 5th grades,
The Governor Morehead School for Blind and Visually Impaired Children

2nd to 5th grades, The Governor Morehead School for Blind and Visually Impaired Children

5th grade, St. Claire Elementary School

3rd to 5th grades, Fremont Elementary School

3rd and 5th grades, Derita Elementary School, in partnership with the Charlotte World Affairs Council

They wear different color clothing like red, black, green, and yellow. The sky is light blue, green grass, and beautiful living animals and plants. Their homes are mainly in pentagon shapes and are made of straw. It is a very clean and healthy place. I would go outside and feed the birds, water the flowers, and enjoy our clean environment.

—*Sherelle Holley, 5th grade, Colerain Elementary School*

3rd Grade, Banner Elk Elementary School

The paradise is like a hundred bottles of perfume just opening. The pond is like a sapphire glistening. The people are blue and green and are like silk to the touch. The ocean is like a dream singing songs of an unknown language. The sun is a bucket of dreams waiting patiently to be dreamt. Xanadu is a wonderful place full of love and kindness. I love Xanadu.

—Margaret Spellman, 2nd grade, Ira. B. Jones Primary

A Travel Brochure to Xanadu

If you are bored where you are . . . Xanadu is just the place for you. The people in Xanadu would be very nice to people who come to visit. There is a sun with tattoos and a pond full of pizza waiting to be fished out. There are houses made of Hershey Kisses and a roller coaster made of rainbow ice cream. In the park at Xanadu lives a playful jaguar named Pumpkin. Come relax on the beautiful flower clouds as you watch the ice cream tornado pass by. Your day would be peaceful with no crimes and no fighting. We hope you visit some day.

—Lee Deer, Ben Garris, Missy Johnson, Autumn Manning, Brittany Minton,
   and Alora Williams, 3rd grade, Banner Elk Elementary School

If this was a perfect world, there would be no El Niño! If this was a perfect world, there would be snow on Christmas and it would always be sunny on spring and summer vacations. A perfect world is where every race and gender stand up for one another, and where people believe in the creator of all things and the preserver of life and light.

—Arria Cheeley, 4th grade, Brooks Global Studies

In a perfect world there would be respect, respect for black people, white people, Jews, and every other religion.

In a perfect world there would be justice for all.

. . . .

In a perfect world there would be forgiveness. Forgiveness for mistakes.

That would be a perfect world.

—Joel Bronstein, 4th grade, Elizabeth Seawell Elementary School

The soft sound of the ocean echoes across Xanadu and the seagulls soar through the clouds. I walk through the gentle waters as it flows through my toes. The seashells sparkle as the sunlight reveals their incredible beauty. I walk over to the thousand magical shells and look upon nature's amazing artwork.

—Mason Malone, 5th grade, Speas Elementary School

4th grade, Elizabeth Seawell Elementary School

Artwork on these two pages is by the 3rd grade, A. T. Allen Elementary School

My job will be as a singer. I want to be a singer so I can raise money for my community. I will sing songs that will talk about everything. *If I have to sign a contract, I will not sign it because in small print they will have rules and I might not want to follow them.*

—Lauren Hester, 2nd grade,
Lakewood Elementary School

A perfect world is a place where the Green Bay Packers always win the Super Bowl. Where the Timberwolves and the Lakers win the most championships. Where all people get treated the same way. Where everybody gets free food. A perfect world is a place where everyone has freedom. Where everyone can dunk on a ten-foot basketball goal.

—*Jacob Schommer, 4th grade, Brooks Global Studies*

My job in Xanadu will be as a team coach. I will be nice to my players. I will say play by the heart. We will win all the games. I will coach for my family.

—*Brandon Alford, 2nd grade, Lakewood Elementary School*

2nd to 8th grades, Loaves and Fishes

In Xanadu there are swimming pools behind every house, basketball hoops in every driveway, and treehouses in every backyard. Recreation and fun are top priorities. The people of Xanadu believe in spending time with your family, so they give you vacations whenever you want. In Xanadu all needs are free but wants cost money.

—Dustin Prusik, 4th grade,
Morrisville Elementary School

Shakti for Children in partnership with the Urban Arts Program of South Eastern Efforts Developing Sustainable Spaces, Inc. (S.E.E.D.S.)

There is peace in Xanadu. You know everything you need to know when you are born so there aren't any schools. . . . There are no tobacco companies and the rich give to the poor. There are lots of pets. Everybody has dogs, cats, and goats.

—Brooks Tellekamp, 3rd grade,
Banner Elk Elementary School

A world of friends • Catch waves in the afternoon sun

Place of friendship, happiness, and caring • Pleasant

All your dreams come true • Butterflies and flowers

Playing, working, sharing together • No violence • Love

Everyone lives in peace • Candy volcano • Respect

No pollution • No monsters under the bed • Singing

5th grade, Elmhurst Elementary School

To live in Xanadu is to ride horses into the sunset and to catch waves in the afternoon's hot sun. They have great piers for fishing, and if you don't fish there is plenty of fun. You can visit the volcano that spits out candy. It's plenty of fun hiking the ice-capped mountains. Then at night, you can kick back, relax, and watch Monday night football.

—Jenna Langston, 5th grade, Elmhurst Elementary School

Our Day at Xanadu

It was a hot day and it was even hotter in our art class. Mrs. Bassett, our art teacher, was talking about Xanadu. We were making a mural of it. When I went to put what I had done about Xanadu, I was sucked in it. Mrs. Bassett knew I was in Xanadu, so she called everybody and off! They were in Xanadu, too.

Xanadu was a small country. But I didn't care. I was only surprised to see all the people from different countries and states. Everyone there was kind and helpful, and they were very respectful. They showed me around to all the different places of Xanadu.

After one day at Xanadu, we were back in the hot classroom. But thinking about Xanadu's pleasant climate made me feel pleasant.

—Mahitha Rajendran, 4th grade,
A. B. Combs Elementary School

4th grade, A. B. Combs Elementary School

My imaginary land would have lots of things like a magical forest, a big waterfall that sings, and lots of other magical things. I would have lots of flowers, animals, and horses that fly.

—Victoria Bullard, 5th grade,
Pembroke Elementary School

4th and 5th grades,
Ansonville Elementary
School

4th grade, Knotts Island
Elementary School

5th grade, W. G. Pearson Elementary School

Xanadu is a place where homes are very colorful and made of candy. It is very calm and relaxing there. It is so peaceful there, when you left your house you wouldn't have to lock your door. My favorite thing to do on a Saturday would be to eat a hole in my house, then fix it.

—Synovia Smith, 5th grade, W. G. Pearson Elementary School

3rd grade, G. W. Bullock Elementary School

Xanadu is a place where you can share your
thoughts, feelings, and opinions with no one to laugh
and tease you about them.

—*Allie Rogers, 5th grade, Elmhurst Elementary School*

5th grade, Nathaniel Alexander Elementary at Governors' Village, in partnership with the Charlotte World Affairs Council

In a perfect world . . . everybody donates half of their salary from work to save the endangered species.

—*Jesse Miller, 4th grade, Elizabeth Seawell Elementary School*

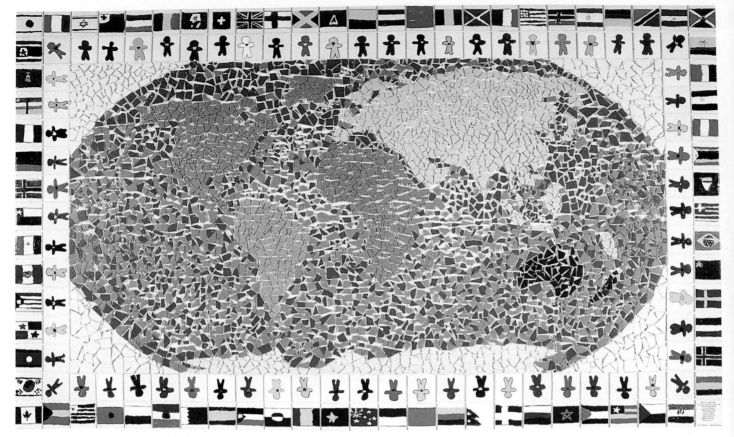

4th grade, Brooks Global Studies

My Xanadu has peace in the world.
Girls can go outside without getting hurt. And
boys can walk down the street without getting
shot.

—*LaToya Cunningham, 5th grade,*

Nathaniel Alexander Elementary at Governors' Village

4th grade, Zeb Vance Elementary School

Xanadu is a place of love and peace.

Xanadu is a place for all.

Xanadu is a place for angels and of beautiful smiles.

Xanadu is a place for hearts of brotherhood and sisterhood.

Xanadu is a place where animals smile and where the sun is happy.

Xanadu is a place where the sharks are glad to be in the ocean.

—Jaiyde Moneyham, 5th grade, W. G. Pearson Elementary School

My imaginary home Xanadu would be filled with happy people. Flowers would cover the land and spring would never end. There would be no drugs. The color of your skin wouldn't matter. Everyone would be treated equally and niceness would overcome meanness.

—*Ashley Hunt, 5th grade, Pembroke Elementary School*

The perfect place to live is under the bed. It's in the dark. You can eat cookies all day. And drink Kool Aid.

—*Sophie Bell, 3rd grade, Forest View Elementary School*

Xanadu is a place of peace and love, where people will respect you and love you. A perfect place to live is a sunflower house, where music follows you along the way.

—*Jasmina Nogo, 3rd grade, Forest View Elementary School*

3rd and 4th grades, Forest View Elementary School

1st grade, Peachtree Elementary School

The perfect place to live in would be a place with pollution-free waters and land. There would be no war and every child would have a mom and dad. A place like this would be a much safer place for everyone to live. If every child had a mother and father, there would be love and happiness all through the air. There would be a lot of family traditions. Children would have their parents to look to for advice.

—Courtney Swoope, 4th grade, Knotts Island Elementary School

Reflections

Maya Ajmera and Olateju Omolodun

One might ask, "Why did you pick Xanadu to be the name of the imaginary place? Why not some other groovy-sounding word?" In 1995, when we were composing **SHAKTI** for Children's first book, *Children from Australia to Zimbabwe*, the concept seemed easy enough: a country for every letter of the alphabet. However, there was one glitch. What to do about X? There is no country that begins with the letter X.

We seriously thought that the project was doomed, until we remembered Samuel Taylor Coleridge's poem "Kubla Khan," "In Xanadu did Kubla Khan / A stately pleasure dome decree. . . ." Xanadu was, according to old travelers' tales, a city where the great thirteenth-century mongol emperor, Kublai Khan, built a stately palace. So, we thought, why not make Xanadu the magical imaginary country in *Children from Australia to Zimbabwe?* And why not let children define it? We piloted the Xanadu Project in schools and community-based organizations in Durham, North Carolina. At Forest View Elementary School, with the guidance of art teacher Marylu Flowers, 150 third- and fourth-grade students from diverse cultures and backgrounds wrote descriptions of their vision of Xanadu and created a spectacular ten-foot-by-ten-foot mural for *Children from Australia to Zimbabwe.* The mural and writings were the perfect finishing touch for a book devoted to the celebration of children's lives around the world.

To our pleasant surprise, the Forest View Xanadu mural began a life of its own. It was displayed in many places in the Triangle area, including the Duke University Museum of Art and the state legislature, as well as being featured on National Public Radio. Dr. John Hope Franklin spoke to the Forest View students at a public reception about his own Xanadu. And over the past several years, Dr. Franklin has become **SHAKTI** for Children's sage, providing us with insight and wisdom about that ideal place called Xanadu. His involvement led us to ask him to share his story about Xanadu for this book.

We began to receive inquiries from other teachers who were interested in pursuing a Xanadu Project in their schools. Without knowing it, we had stumbled upon a program that fit perfectly with **SHAKTI** for Children's mission to teach children to value diversity and to grow into productive, caring citizens of the world. Not only did we feel that the Xanadu Project could enhance relations among diverse groups of children, but we saw that it could also be an important character-building exercise. What we had learned from previous partnerships helped us to develop criteria that would give children the opportunity to

- Express their dreams for the future, visually and orally
- Reflect on living in a place made up of diverse peoples and learn of the similarities that connect them to children everywhere—emotions, relationships, and activities
- Help children understand community and its virtues of trust, respect, and cooperation
- Identify and choose the elements of an imaginary place
- Work together toward a common goal and learn about the benefits of teamwork
- Improve their painting, drawing, compositional, and writing skills
- Receive recognition from the community for their work.

As this project expanded, we saw several common themes emerging in the children's vision of Xanadu. Their artwork and writings reflect a need for a clean environment and a need to honor all life—our own and the life of many animals that inhabit our earth. They reflect love, which is the foundation for humanity, and the knowledge that feeling safe and having a home are basic needs.

The many Xanadus that children have created give all of us the impetus to freely imagine a perfect place to live. Candy-shooting volcanoes, gingerbread houses, and purple and green people exist right along with respect, peace, and love in their imaginary places. Why shouldn't they? Children are unhindered by the limitations adults place on themselves. Their artwork and writings pose a question; if we are indeed striving for communities of justice, equality, and respect, shouldn't our spirits be imaginative and creative? As the children imagine sunflower homes, the Statue of Liberty lounging in a fountain, or several climates existing in one environment, they are in fact asking us to step outside of our boxes and dream.

When we visited schools working on the project in North Carolina, we asked students and teachers what they had learned in the process of creating their Xanadu. We heard from teachers how the qualities of Xanadu came to life in their classrooms. The students became a community that held the virtues of trust, respect, and cooperation as they molded and shaped their community physically and morally. One art teacher who chose her fourth-grade classes for the project said she thought the children wouldn't work well as a team. However, she said, "because of the subject matter and the way we discussed Xanadu, they were more open to working together and accepting of each other's ideas." Another art teacher commented, "The most enjoyable part for me was watching them add things to the original idea. It was like watching one child throw an idea downfield and another child catch it and score a touchdown with it." Some students came up with really great ideas, some drew very well, some were careful painters, some tackled the composition of the land (city and regional planning, we may call it), and everyone gave support and encouragement. Isn't that how all communities should be? Xanadu was no longer imaginary in the classroom; it became real.

So what other things did we learn? Some of the artwork reflects the colors and cultures of many different people and some do not. Some of the children's work demonstrated how much multicultural education is needed in the classroom and how it must aim toward breaking down stereotypes. We learned that diversity is not only about culture or ethnicity but includes environmental and social perspectives as well. It seemed natural that some Xanadus incorporated real elements from the children's natural environments, as in Knotts Island and Banner Elk. Peachtree Elementary School, located in Murphy in Cherokee County, is surrounded by the Smoky Mountains; not surprisingly, the Xanadu created by the Peachtree students reflected a community nestled in the mountains. On the other hand, the Xanadu created by children of A. B. Combs Elementary School in Raleigh in Wake County, depicted a very busy and urban scene, reflecting the capital of North Carolina. Some Xanadus reflected the diversity of the student body, as we saw in the creations of students in A. T. Allen, Combs, Elizabeth Seawell, Forest View, and Elmhurst elementary schools.

One marvelous Xanadu was created by students at the Governor Morehead School for Blind and Visually Impaired Children. Their Xanadu can be touched— there are soft feathers on the bird sitting on its straw nest atop a Peppermint Patty tree. We saw tremendous diversity in the artistic media used on these projects. Xanadus have been created as quilts, as cut-paper collages, tile mosaics, and acrylic on canvas or bed sheets; one Xanadu was created to look like a view through a window. They have been influenced by the collages of Romare Bearden and the quilts of Faith Ringgold. The creative possibilities for Xanadu are endless, and we foresee that it will continue to take many forms as the vision spreads to children and teachers across the country and around the world.

Because children's creativity should be celebrated and recognized, many Xanadus will be showcased in public places in North Carolina and beyond. In public libraries and university museums, in state legislatures and the media, Xanadus and their creators will be honored for their work. One day, some of these Xanadus may be showcased at the Library of Congress or the United Nations. In keeping with this spirit, we honor the students and teachers and their communities for their leadership and commitment to Xanadu.

Artwork and writings were obtained from the following schools:

A. B. Combs Elementary School, Raleigh, Wake County. *Art Teacher:* Martha Bassett.
Students: Yussuf Abdel-aleem, Yemi Adebiyi, Natasha Alexander, Josh Allen, Andrea Badegtt, Morgan Baltrus, Idahlia Bayoumi, Jeff Blair, Robbie Beasley, Nick Brust, Michelle Campen, Christopher Castro-Rapple, Brandy Clack-Wilson, Cory Coleman, Brittany Cowan, Samuel Corbett, Kaycee Cross, Rachel Crowder, Natasha Cupeles, Lee Davis, Shane Davis, Mario DeHaro, Jeffrey Despain, Calie Edmonds, Nadeem Elborno, Sarah Faulkner, Glen Fournier, Anne Fraser, Chris Geddis, Johan Gilarranz, Brandy Griffin, Jonathan Harris, Stephen Hudson, Itzel Izquierdo, Matthew Jackson, Antwon Jones, Caitlin Jones, Christopher Jordan, Brian Koch, Elizabeth Lamb, Oliver Madden, Anthony Lee, Brenda McDaniel, Toby Mele, Jacob Murphy, Amanda Nichols, Bridgit O'Donnell, Joseph Ofodile, Jessica Penny, Khrystal Pettiford, Ashley Poole, Kelsey Poorman, Sara Posey, Syeda Quadri, Mahitha Rajendran, Brooke Ramsey, Aarthi Ravichander, Rosemary Reeves, Jessica Rubinoff, Mohammad Shad, Taylor Shanklin, Allison Silsbee, Carol Son, Prakash Subramanian, Cole Stephenson, Joseph Sutton, Scott Sweeney, Michele Vanderlip, Maria Vozzo, Billy Williams, Alex Wolff-Tripp, Anna Woodruff, Ziyad Yaghi, and Keenan Yokell. *Fourth-Grade Teachers:* Ron Carter, Lisa Fletcher, Pat Montague, and Anne Watson. *Photograph taken by* Charles Gupton Photography.

Ansonville Elementary School, Ansonville, Anson County. *Art Teacher:* Stacy Ferguson. *Students:* Kamisha Allen, Travis Beachum, Olandus Blankeney, Jamie Bowman, Joel Brewer, Travis Cowick, Eryn Edwards, Stephanie Flower, Chantal Green, Carrie Hamilton, Dagney Horne, Tia Alexandrea Horne, Kyle Johnson, Cory King, Lauren Kirby, Erica Kiser, David Leak, Tony Ledbetter, Shequilla Lisenby, Janice Little, Kelicia Little, Lamonica Massey, Marvin Medley, Adam Moore, Beverly Morris, Brian Pruitt, Lamorris Rivers, Dinisha Rorie, Sean Sellers, Maleah Sikes, Sargon Smith, Corissa Steele, Latavia Sturdivant, Priscilla Sturdivant, Corderrick Teal, Jacob Thomas, Wade Thomas, Hollie Treadaway, Chasity Tucker, Cardaron Tyson, Matthew Tyson, Katondra Wall, Sky Watkins, Kevin White, Samuel Williams, and Kou Xiong. *Photograph taken by* Charles Allison.

A. T. Allen Elementary School, Concord, Cabarrus County. *Art Teacher:* Joyce Roberts. *Project Coordinator:* Cindy Scott, Assistant Principal of Instruction. *Students:* Alex Anderson, Claudia Arciga, Phillip Atkinson, Heather Betters, Belaney Beyene, Austin Billingsley, Alisha Blackwelder, Kristen Brines, Jaison Brooks, Josh Brooks, Matthew Brown, Lashonda Cannon, Shere Carson, Robin Christy, Laura Cochran, Nicole Connelly, Kayla Cook, Megan Danforth, Amanda Deese, Anthony Dennis, Quentin Dulaney, Travis Elkins, Kristin Foster, Amy Funderburk, Brittany Gentle, Ronnie Given, Renay Gray, Ashley Green, Curtina Grier, Aaron Halbeisen, Christy Hayes, Daniel Helle, Ashleigh Helms, Josh Hendricks, Jose Hernandez, Brittney Hodnett, Brenton Hopkins, Johnny Hullet, Matthew Isenhour, Josh Jackson, Stephanie Keller, Ashley Kepley, Shane Kindley, Shirmarka Lynch, Chelsea Mauldin, Amber McDonald, Jeremy McGlynn, Erika Melendez, Raudel Moreno, Brittany Moser, Christy Newton, Stephen O'Reilly, Joshua Owen, Christen Patterson, Daniell Petrea, Dameon Pharr, Rashard Propst, Dennis Schoenfeld, Christian Serrano, Jamey Sexton, Chet Sherrife, Jonathan Smith, Kimberly Smith, Megan Smith, Juan Solis, Tecoya Stafford, Hannah Svenkerud, Chris Tallent, Alex Torres, Heather Troutman, Chance Vredenburg, Quentin Wallace, Adam Williams, Jennifer Williams, J. C. Whitley, and Matthew Whitley. *Photograph taken by* Brady Lambert.

Banner Elk Elementary School, Banner Elk, Avery County. *Art Teacher:* Stephanie Jones. *Students:* Robin Adams, Julie Arnett, Benjamin Bell, Brett Berry, Cameron Berry, Seth Carriere, Amanda Crump, Lee Deer, Ashley Franklin, Ben Garris, Will Garris, Logan Gentry, Lindsay Harmon, Shane Hayward, Rose Himmelman, Brandon Isenhour, Missy Johnson, Jessica Koerber, Autumn Manning, Brittany Minton, Chealssea Morris, Clare Natali, Jesse Ollis, Jimmy Puckett, Tommy Scully, Heather Shelton, Miles Shipley, Brett Shomaker, Ashley Smith, Josh Stevens, Brooks Tellekamp, Andrew Thompson, Joseph Townsend, Lindsey Townsend, Alora Williams, Matthew Wimberley, and Jimmy Yates. *Third-Grade Teachers:* Edie Ferguson, Diana Love, and Teresa Taylor. *Photograph taken by* Todd L. Bush Photographer.

Brooks Global Studies, Greensboro, Guilford County. *Art Teacher:* Ninette Humber. *Students:* Wyman Apple, Delorea Baker, Megan Beard, Jasmine Bethea, Eric Briggs, Rachael Campbell, Charles Cassell, Arria Cheeley, Victoria Colston-Brooks, Meighan Dally, Liz Davis, Sabrina Davis, Chaz Erwin, Rachel Gaines, Chauncee Garrett, Jamison Gilyard, Ashley Goodwin, Galissia Graves, Adam Gray, Whitney Green, Ashley Guffey, Spencer Hamrick, Laura Hansen, Jennifer Henry, Ashley Isaacs, Eric Jackson, Jeremiah Jenkins, Brittany Lawrence, Tiffany Lewis, Steven Lim, Jonathan Luo, Leann Madtes, Brian Martin, Michael Matulla, Kelvin McCauley, Jessica Means, Rachel Means, Lauren Melton, Lindsey Metzger, Chelsea Miles, Donnie Mitchell, Jahon Nanajl, Whitney Neal, Ayeshan Parker, Lerone Peoples, Marissa Phillips, Zach Piliey, Jessica Pollard, Addison Poole, Brandon Raleigh, Corey Ravenell, Jay Reid, Bradley Reiser, Bradley Russell, Erika Salter, Jacob Schommer, Myles Scott, Alex Smith, Katrina Smith, Jeffrey Solomon, Amber Southern, Alice Stamatakis, Dale Tonkins, Seaton Trotter, Luke Tuck, Brandon Umphrey, Ryan Walker, Chris Weatherly, Mason White, Kelsey Whitehouse, Julie Williams, Zack Woody, Caille Young, and Emily Yount. *Photograph courtesy of* Charlie Lowe.

Derita Elementary School, Charlotte, Mecklenburg County. *Art Teacher:* Sheryl Marinelli. *Project Coordinator:* Donna Devereaux, Assistant Director, Charlotte World Affairs Council. *Students:* Thomas Boriboun, Courtney Browne, Teddie Fletcher, Jeffrey Glenn, Crystal Hill, Latavia Hollande, Allison Jones, India Jones, Emily Kaiser, Chelsea Meffert, Kate Ramage, Amber Richardson, David Roberts, Scottie Roberts, Sam Ruchti, Shayna Shives, Stacie Terry, and Thao-van Thai. *Photograph taken by* Kelly Culpepper Photography.

Elizabeth Seawell Elementary School, Chapel Hill, Orange County. *Art Teacher:* Annie Cramer. *Students:* Ellen Abrams, Travis Allen, Meredith Allred, Kelsie Armentrout, Alisha Atwater, Matthew Ball, Gabriel Barker, Tanya Battye, Clare Baucom, Micheal Berman, Michelle Besterfield, Peter Bohlen, Conor Boland, Joel Bronstein, Maria Callimanis, Miriam Carnick, Charles Clarke, Richard Covach, Montego Crisp, Deryle Daniels, Elizabeth Davis, Marianna Edgerton, Darine El-Sourady, William Farley, Donald Farrow, D'marrsaan Foster, Anne Gauthier, Keyona Gibson, Jeffrey Giersbrook, Jordan Gottschalk, Brian Graham, Garrett Grubb, Jennie Hardin, Russell Hawkins, Nicci Hayes, Tiarra Headen, Jeffrey Hertzberg, Samantha Hill, Alexander Hu, Antonio Jackson, Rodrico Jackson, Matthew Jenkins, Matthew Johnson, Catherine Jones, Erin Kabrick, Tyler Kaufman, Tim Kihlstrom, Peter Kostin, Kimberly Lurie, Susanna Mage, Ricky Maki, Christopher Manning, Samantha Marcheschi, Craig Marimpietri, Katharine Markley, Emily McAdams, Megan McCray, Jesse Miller, Luke Miller, Maura Mohler, Shaneal Moore, Brett Moran, Elsa Offenbacher, John Palumbo, Julie Peck, Samantha Peckham, Ryan Peiffer, John Pierson, Danielle Plesser, Maher Powers, Mary Ann Pressley, Allison Price, Emily Privette, Honre Purefoy, Niket Ram, Mathias Rhoads, Demeisha Roberson, Trevor Robinson, Abigail Rosenberg, Theoren Smith, Philip Spencer, Tana Stewart, Kim Tripp, Elise Valla, Sarah Van der Horst, Jason Wang, Jordan Weber, Allison Weinstock, Glen Wheeler, Ben Wiener, Jordan Williams, Matt Williams, Whitney Wright, Samuel Wurzelmann, and Jessica Zaleon. *Fourth-Grade Teacher:* Esther Mateo-Orr. *Photograph taken by* Photo Quick.

Elmhurst Elementary School, Greenville, Pitt County. *Art Teacher:* Ann Cherry. *Students:* Adam Ballance, Patrick Brock, Kristen Brown, Mallory Carter, Allison Clark, Kelvin Common, Lauren Cox, Brenton Edwards, Meagan Edwards, Meredith Felts, Samantha Frazier, Kyle Gray, Will Griffin, Brittney Grimes, Ashley Gwaltney, Catherine Hathaway, Bryan Hill, Jon Holvedt, Jenna Langston, Amy Li, Sarai Little, Jenna Lindsay, Erika Lozano, Virginia McGraw, Chris Melgar, Brittany Mills, Trey Moye, Kozue Oshika, Allie Rogers, Jennifer Schultz, Ravi Vadlamudi, and Antoinette Walker. *Photograph taken by* Greg Ward/ASAP Photo & Camera

Forest View Elementary School, Durham, Durham County. *Art Teacher:* Marylu Flowers. *1995–96 Community Outreach Coordinator,* **SHAKTI** *for Children:* Vanessa Davis. *Students:* Rashad Aldridge, Gerald Alston, Marcus Anderson, Eric Arendshorst, Ruth Attamack, Alloray Baker, Alphonso Barnes, Allison Bartlett, Germaine Baugh, Jamie Bell, Sophie Bell, Joshua Bennetone, Darius Rorie-Blackmon, Jesica Bonilla, Kalynn Botts, Christopher Breeden, Christopher Briggs, Charlene Broomes, Jeffrey Brown, Patrick Brown, Audrina Bunton, Cassady Burke, Matthew Clayton, Sean Clayton, William Clayton, Joshua Climer, Marlo Cohen, Charlissa Copeland, Marcus Cousin, Robert Crumpler, Christopher

Dadok, Du Dai, Johnny Dang, Shavon Daniel, Taijia Dennis, Bethany Diprete, Sara Dodson, Barrett Donner, Emelia Dunston, Elise Edgerton, Mandel Edwards, Sirgeo Ellis, Yvette Eregie, Jay-ar Foronda, Molly Freeman, Emily Frenzel, Simon Gaddy, Jesse Gellerson, Gregory Gibson, Bettina Goesele, Jennifer Gore, Zachary Gornto, Ta'shanna Gray, Niketa Green, Kyle Griffin, Jessica Hackett, Tyler Harris, Darrell Harris, Tequila Harris, Brittany Hayes, Jessica Henderson, Damon Henry, Sade Henry, Abigail Hernandez, Dante Hill, Alexandria Horne, Paul Huang, Hanna Hwang, Bryce Jenkins, Sabrina Jennette, Katherine Johnston, Jasmyne Jones, Dallas Kegley, Grace Kendall, Jamahl Kennard, Aditya Kher, Seo Kim, Jonathan Lampe, Bilal Lateef, Omayra Lema, Benjamin Leone, Jason Leone, Janice Liu, Syrone Liu, Bryan Lochman, Judithe Louis, Mariam Loynab, Emily Lytle, Brandon Madden, Mary Jane Martin, Hector Maya, Lauren McAskill, Kim McCallum, Sean McCauley, Kempest McEachirn, Rowan Meehan, Lydia Mikhaylyants, Emily Miller, Kathryn Mims, Brian Moran, Anjan Mukherjee, Saif Murad, Randell Murrell, Manuela Navarro, Jasmina Nogo, Alicia Oas, Natishia O'Neal, Onunga Ooro, Ezinne Oputa, Michelle Ostrowski, Jarrell Peak, Kevin Pearlstein, Travis Peele, Nicholas Philbrick, Christina Quintano, Brandon Rabb, Erik Ramires, Joshua Rivera, Natalie Rossman, Donald Rush, Dylan Russell, Danna Saleh, Taylor Savage, Karthik Sekar, Anastassia Sharpe, Kevin Shumaker, Jesse Shumate, Jeffrey Smith, Solomon Tate, Mario Tedder, Kendra Tee, Abdramane Traore, Natalie Turkaly, Kissel Valencia, Samuel Valencia, Jose Velazquez, Claire Walker, Andre Ward, Latia Ward, Whitney Wicker, Adriene Williams, Jason Williams, Tishonda Williams, Shamecka Williamson, Evan Witkowski, Hayley Wood, Teshana Young, and Chenwei Zhang. *Photograph taken by* Brady Lambert.

Fremont Elementary School, Fremont, Wayne County. *Art Teacher:* Joy Vinson. *Students:* Terell Coley, Garrett Davis, Taylor Davis, Brandon Haynes, Mario Holmes, Aaron Nelson, Ben Nelson, Alex Newsome, Shayne Paul, Antre Reid, Patrick Smith, Leiren Tillman, Chelsea Vinson, and Lamada Williams. *Photograph taken by* John Feely/*Fremont News Leader.*

The Governor Morehead School for Blind and Visually Impaired Children, Raleigh, Wake County. *Art Teacher:* Liz List. *Students:* Daria Bannerman, Ebonie Boatwright, Buddy Chavis, Andrew Daniels, Daniel Gore, Luke Huntley, Ebony Johnson, and La'Teaya Lee. *Photograph taken by* Brady Lambert.

G. W. Bullock Elementary School, Rocky Mount, Edgecombe County. *Advanced Gifted Teacher:* Susan Warren. *Art Teacher:* Pat Daughteridge. *Students:* Makeysa Coley, Kristen Everett, Jazman Hines, Lynsy Howard, Brandon Lyons, Kabryn Mattison, Matthew McFarlin, Andy Perry, Ashley Rhodes, Sarah Robbins, Christopher Whichard, Monique Williams, and Josh Young. *Photograph taken by* Gardner Photography.

G. W. Carver Elementary School, Pinetops, Edgecombe County. *Advanced Gifted Teacher:* Susan Warren. *Art Teacher:* Millie Holloman. *Art Interns:* Jennifer Ganzel, Kristen Napier. *Students:* Tara Allen, Emily Briley, Candid Cobb, Hillary Corbett, Tiara Epps, Mario Immediato, Holly Lancaster, Kendra Stallings, Veniece Staton, Simone Thigpen, Kristin Webb, Rebecca Webb, and Justin Whitley. *Photograph taken by* Gardner Photography.

Knotts Island Elementary School, Knotts Island, Currituck County. *Art Teachers:* Gary Freeman and Virginia Schwallen. *Students:* Eddie Allen, Cassie Baines, Stephen Childress, Benjamin Dinkel, Kenny Golden, Herbert Gygi, Cara Hall, Kimberly Hermann, Amber Keement, Patricia Montes, Cory Parker, Ashley Potter, Brandon Riddle, Ashley Robinson, Nichole Snipes, Sarah Spevack, Courtney Swoope, Jessica Truskowski, Madisan Vakos, Laura Wallace, and Shannon Weekley. *Photograph taken by* Brady Lambert.

Loaves and Fishes, Raleigh, Wake County. *Project Coordinators:* Sarah Cooper, Director of Youth Programs, and Jen Davis, Director of Children's Programs. *1997–98 Director of Community Education, SHAKTI for Children:* Olateju Omolodun. *Students:* Archie Austin, Crishounda Burnett, Travis Burt, Reggie Faison, Cornelius Faison, Kiosha Griffin, Tewanda Griffin, Brandon Griffis, Kendra Griffis, Tachelle Griffis, Nina Haywood, Anthony Hinton, Cynquita Jeffreys, Latasha Jeffreys, Chris Jolly, Fenton Jolly, Latrail McCoy, Ebony Mercer, Markcus Riley, Ricco Roberston, Shan Robinson, Quintin Signal, Eddie Smith, Mario Thorpe, Josh Tuck, Shaquanna Williams, and Meme Wright. *Photograph taken by* Brady Lambert.

Nathaniel Alexander Elementary at Governors' Village, Charlotte, Mecklenburg County. *Art Teacher:* Loretta Banner, *Project Coordinator:* Donna Devereaux, Assistant Director, Charlotte World Affairs Council. *Students:* Bobby Adden, Ryan Bell, Dylan Carney, LaToya Cunningham, Keyes Dickson, Rachel Estes, Nichole Garren, Katie Henry, Chrystina Hoffman, Courtney Jones, Amanda Judge, Doris Kilgo, Laonzo Long, George Maddox, Zack O'Brien, Charles Oates, Aaron Royal, T. J. Stephens, Jamie Troutman, Anh Vuong, Ivy Wells, and Ryan Wilson. *Photograph taken by* Kelly Culpepper Photography.

Peachtree Elementary School, Murphy, Cherokee County. *Art Teacher:* Laurie Weinkle. *Students:* Dakota Beaver, Heather Bradshaw, Tabitha Day, Brandi Garrett, Malcolm Gruber, Amity Ledford, Dustin Lingerfelt, Dalton Mallonee, Autumn McClure, Adrian Roberson, Amberly Stanford, Katie Stilwell, Christopher Taylor, and Hannah Ulrikson. *Photograph taken by* Hawkins Photography.

S.E.E.D.S., Durham, Durham, County. *Project Coordinator:* Cayman Lee, Urban Arts Program. *1995–96 Community Outreach Coordinator, SHAKTI for Children:* Vanessa Davis. *Students:* Christopher Beasley, Antonio Edwards, Dominique Edwards, Alex McKiver, Jamarcus Reams, Oshea Reams, Shaquana Reams, D'Mario Smith, and Steven Smith. *Photograph taken by* Brady Lambert.

St. Claire Elementary School, Sanford, Lee County. *Art Teacher:* Ron Noles. *Students:* Elizabeth Beal, Richard Feindel, Elisabeth Griffin, Eric Mangum, Tiffany Mellete, Whitney Phillips, Vanessa Reeder, and Caitlin Taaffe. *Photograph courtesy of* Karl Straub.

W. G. Pearson Elementary School, Durham, Durham County. *Art Teacher:* Susan Siravo. *1996–97 Community Outreach Coordinator, SHAKTI for Children:* Olateju Omolodun. *Students:* Kadisha A. Belk, Darrius D. Blanding, Shannon M. Boyd, Catrina R. Carr, Tommy Darren China, Sykrina Dale, Victoria L. Dingle, Sierra D. Dunn, Estora Karl Ensley, Kenyatta Antoi Frye, Starr Frye, Javonda N. Fullard, Carma Fuller, Shedrrick R. Gibbs, Ashley D. Harris, Mario J. Herron, Crystal D. Hodges, Krystal N. Holman, Darius Howell, Michael A. Hudson, Miriam Alise Ingram, Zachary W. Jeffers, Joshua Lamont Johnson, Tequila Jones, Bradley Kearney, K'mmando Deyon Latta, Shawntia F. Lee, Princess Liles, Quinton Lamont Long, Rodriquez Lowe, Kanisha S. Madison, Jerry Martin, Jharmick L. Meeks, Larrico D. McBride, Latasha McGilberry, Micheal McLaurin, Brandon McLaurin, Lashonda McLean, Maurice A. McNeil, Keith Antonio McNeil, Jaiyde L. Moneyham, Phillipe A. Parker, Quenna N. Poole, Franklin Revels, Jessica Robertson, Anaees Robinson, Sharkera A. Royster, Ashley Rorie, Donta' L. Ruffin, Erica S. Sanders, Traynita M. Scott, Natasha S. Smith, Synovia D. Smith, Latorria M. Street, Michael J. Strudwick, Kimberly Turner, Dwight N. Turrentine, Dezmond R. Williams, and Ebony M. Williams. *Photograph taken by* Brady Lambert.

Zeb Vance Elementary School, Kittrell, Vance County. *Art Teacher:* Lisa Phillips. *Students:* Sherri Alston, Jermill Blacknall, Niki Bond, Lillian Dawson, Lauren Deans, Heather Dinwiddie, Brandon Edwards, Cameron Ellington, Brandon Hayes, Leah Hendrix, Chris Hock, Ashley Hudgins, Stephanie Maynard, Jamie McGhee, Angel Owens, Montrell Person, Randi Rollings, Anna Twisdale, Ashley Watson, Robbie Whitbey, and Tiffany Wright. *Fourth-Grade Language Arts Teacher:* Judy Lassiter. *Photograph taken by* Brady Lambert.

Writings were obtained from the following schools:

Colerain Elementary School, Colerain, Bertie County
Ira B. Jones Primary School, Asheville, Buncombe County
Lakewood Elementary School, Durham, Durham County
Morrisville Elementary School, Moorisville, Wake County
Pembroke Elementary School, Pembroke, Robeson County
Speas Elementary School, Winston-Salem, Forsyth County

Special Thanks to:

The 1995–1997 William C. Friday Fellows of the Citizenship Project; Donna Devereaux and Jennifer Watson-Roberts of the Charlotte World Affairs Council; editors Alexa Dilworth and Maura High; Anne Theilgard of Kachergis Book Design, Inc.; **SHAKTI** for Children Board of Directors.

Maya Ajmera is the founder and executive director of **SHAKTI** for Children, a nonprofit organization committed to teaching children to value diversity and to grow into productive, caring citizens of the world. Raised in Greenville, North Carolina, she received a bachelor's degree from Bryn Mawr College and a master's degree in public policy from the Sanford Institute of Public Policy at Duke University. She is the coauthor of several **SHAKTI** for Children Books, including *Children from Australia to Zimbabwe* with Anna Rhesa Versola and *To Be a Kid* with John Ivanko. She is the recipient of the 1995–1997 William C. Friday Fellowship for Human Relations of North Carolina.

Olateju Omolodun is the Director of Community Education of **SHAKTI** for Children. A native of Nigeria and raised in Raleigh, North Carolina, Ms. Omolodun received her bachelor's degree in communications from the University of North Carolina at Chapel Hill. From 1996–97, she was a North Carolina Public Ally. She is a poet and an artistic performer.

Dr. John Hope Franklin is a teacher, historian, scholar, writer, and activist. He is the James B. Duke Professor Emeritus of History at Duke University. The author of many books, including the classic *From Slavery to Freedom: A History of African-Americans, The Free Negro in North Carolina*, he is considered a founding father of African American history. Dr. Franklin provided Supreme Court Justice Thurgood Marshall with critical historical research for the landmark case of *Brown v. Board of Education*.

A native of Oklahoma, Dr. Franklin graduated from Fisk University and Harvard University. He has taught at a number of institutions, including North Carolina Central University, St. Augustine College, Howard University, Brooklyn College, and the University of Chicago. He has also taught in many different countries, including Australia, the former Soviet Union, the United Kingdom, and China. Dr. Franklin has received over 110 honorary degrees.

Dr. Franklin was the recipient of the 1995 Presidential Medal of Freedom, awarded by President Clinton. He also served as chairman of the advisory board for One America: The President's Initiative on Race. Dr. Franklin makes his home with his family in Durham, North Carolina. As a teacher, historian, scholar, writer, activist, and avid lover of orchids, Dr. Franklin has inspired many people to follow their dreams and visions.

Artwork, Front Cover: © 1997–1998 G.W. Carver Elementary School, Pinetops, North Carolina, USA. *Title Page:* © 1996–1997 A.T. Allen Elementary School, Third Grade Classes, Concord, North Carolina, USA. *Pages 2 and 3:* © 1996–1997 A.T. Allen Elementary School, Third Grade Classes, Concord, North Carolina, USA. *Page 5:* © 1997–1998 Governor Morehead School, Raleigh, North Carolina, USA, *Page 6:* © 1997–1998 Fremont Elementary School, Fremont, North Carolina, USA., and © 1997–1998 St. Claire Elementary School, Sanford, North Carolina, USA. *Page 7:* © 1997–1998 Derita Elementary School, Charlotte, North Carolina, USA. *Pages 8 and 9:* © 1997–1998 Banner Elk Elementary School, Banner Elk, North Carolina, USA. *Page 11:* © 1997–1998 Elizabeth Seawell Elementary School, Chapel Hill, North Carolina, USA. *Pages 12 and 13:* © 1996–1997 A.T. Allen Elementary School, Third Grade Classes, Concord, North Carolina, USA. *Page 14:* © 1997 Loaves and Fishes and **SHAKTI** for Children, Raleigh, North Carolina, USA, and © 1996 S.E.E.D.S. and **SHAKTI** for Children, Durham, North Carolina, USA. *Page 15:* © 1997–1998 Elmhurst Elementary School, Greenville, North Carolina, USA. *Page 16:* © 1997–1998 Ansonville Elementary School, Ansonville, North Carolina, USA, and © 1997–1998 Knotts Island Elementary School, Knotts Island, North Carolina, USA. *Page 17:* © 1996–1997 W.G. Pearson Elementary School, Fifth Grade Classes and **SHAKTI** for Children, Durham, North Carolina, USA. *Pages 18 and 19:* © 1997–1998 A.B. Combs Elementary School, Raleigh, North Carolina, USA. *Page 20:* © 1997–1998 G.W. Bullock Elementary School, Rocky Mount, North Carolina, USA. *Page 21:* © 1997–1998 Nathaniel Alexander Elementary at Governors' Village, Charlotte, North Carolina, USA. *Page 22:* © 1997–1998 Brooks Global, Greensboro, North Carolina, USA. *Page 23:* © 1997–98 Zeb Vance Elementary School, Kittrell, North Carolina, USA. *Page 25:* © 1995–1996 Forest View Elementary, Third-Grade and Third/Fourth-Grade combination classes and **SHAKTI** for Children, Durham, North Carolina, USA. *Page 26:* © 1997–98 Peachtree Elementary School, Murphy, North Carolina, USA.

Publisher's Cataloging-in-Publication Data
Xanadu, the imaginary place : a showcase of artwork and writings by North Carolina's children / with a story by John Hope Franklin ; edited by Maya Ajmera and Olateju Omolodun. — 1st ed.
    p. cm.
    ISBN 0-9651722-2-8 (cloth)—ISBN 0-9651722-3-6 (pbk.)
    SUMMARY: North Carolina children describe and draw their individual visions of a perfect place in which to live.

    1. Utopias—Juvenile literature. 2. Utopias—Pictoral works—Juvenile literature. I. Ajmera, Maya. II. Omolodun, Olateju. III. Franklin, John Hope, 1915–
    HX810.X36 1998   321'.07
                QB198-1025

Printed in South Korea
10 9 8 7 6 5 4 3 2 1

Xanadu was designed and composed in Monotype's Columbus by Kachergis Book Design, Pittsboro, North Carolina. This book was separated, printed, and bound by Sung In Printing, Inc., South Korea.